Trevor Haddrell
2002

Panoramic Bristol

Panoramic Bristol

fifty engravings and linocuts

TREVOR HADDRELL

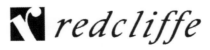 redcliffe

First published in 2002 by Redcliffe Press Ltd.
   81g Pembroke Road, Bristol BS8 3EA
   0117 973 7207

© engravings and text: Trevor Haddrell
   Woodwell Cottage, White Hart Steps
   Clifton Wood Bristol BS8 4TQ
   0117 929 8363

   ISBN 1 900178 64 8

British Library Cataloguing-in-Publication Data.
A catalogue record for this book is available from the British Library.

Typeset and designed by Stephen Morris Communications, smc@freeuk.com
and printed by HSW Print, Tonypandy, Rhondda

CONTENTS

For John and Rachel
with
love and thanks

August 2002

Introduction

PAINTER AND PRINT-MAKER TREVOR HADDRELL was born in Rotherham, South Yorkshire and moved south to train as an Art & Design teacher at Bath Academy of Art, Corsham when Clifford Ellis was the principal there. He later completed a BA Honours degree through the Open University. He taught art at Ashton Park School, Bristol from 1967, eventually becoming head of department. He then moved to Clifton High School as Head of Art & Design in 1984 and retired from teaching in 2000.

Over the years, Trevor Haddrell has had many shared and one-man shows of paintings, drawings and relief prints at a number of local venues. He has exhibited several times in the three-yearly National Print shows at the Royal West of England Academy, winning a prize for a panoramic print of Bristol Docks in 1997. He also exhibits regularly with the Society of Wood Engravers. His work is in many private collections, in the permanent collection of Bristol Museum and Art Gallery, and the Theatre Collection of Bristol University.

The artist writes:

'I always felt, throughout my years as a schoolteacher, that it was important to practise what I preached. I took part in a number of exhibitions over the years. My interest in producing my own work was deep and serious and, I believe, enriched my teaching. I tended to concentrate on drawings and watercolours for most of this time and the city provided me with most of my subject matter.

Bristol has always given much stimulus to my work but I have also had a long and enduring love of Venice which I visit regularly, usually alone so that I can spend all day and every day drawing and painting. In both cities, I tend to focus on quirky juxtapositions of various styles of architecture, roof-scapes and reflections in water and glass.

'In about 1993, I began to explore relief print-making processes more thoroughly, initially for teaching purposes. (It actually came about when a new floor was laid in the Art Room at the school where I was teaching and I could not bear to see all the vinyl off-cuts being thrown out when it was done.) Relief printing has become a major part of my artistic out-put over the past few years. I have tended to specialise in black and white engraving techniques, though I have done some experiments with coloured prints, too, using several over-printed blocks in the Japanese manner.

'I have developed an abiding interest in Japanese prints, particularly those concentrating on landscape by artists such as Hokusai and Hiroshige. I also admire the work of many British wood-engravers, especially Eric Ravilious, Gertrude Hermes, John Farleigh and Blair Hughes-Stanton'.

The Panorama of Bristol prints

This set of 50 engravings and linocuts of Bristol has been the first major commission I have undertaken since I retired from teaching in July 2000. Some of the prints were produced as far back as 1995 but the majority have been made in the past year or so especially for this book.

I have tried to give a personal view of aspects of the city of particular interest to me. Many of the designs contain elements which will be familiar to anyone who knows the city even slightly, but I have attempted to view most of the subjects from unusual vantage points which will, I hope, offer some new perspectives on the city.

The prints are loosely grouped into four main sections: the Docks; Clifton and Clifton Wood; Brandon Hill and Environs, and Around the City Centre and Beyond. Each section contains subjects which can been seen in the sequence in which they appear, in four walks around those different areas of the city. The captions give the exact viewing point I took for each design.

Though I have had to pause to lament, here and there, certain things which have been lost to us over the thirty years I have lived in Bristol, my overall intention in these prints has been to celebrate the vitality and variety which can be seen and felt in our city.

The techniques used

These designs are based on drawings done from observation.
The original prints, from which the reproductions in this book were made, were
produced by a relief print-making process similar to that used for wood engravings.

For most of them, traditional wood-engraving tools were used, sometimes combined with fine lino-cutting gouges, but the designs were engraved on to smooth vinyl blocks, not wood or lino. This means the prints could be large-scale when necessary but they could also be quite delicately engraved to give the effect of mid-tones and fine detail. Wherever prints exploit a range of tones in this way, they are referred to as engravings in the captions which accompany the illustrations.

Wherever only lino-cutting gouges were used, as in some of the earliest prints, these are referred to, for convenience, as lino-cuts even though vinyl, not lino, was used for the blocks. These prints are typified by bold cutting, without great detail. The designs are made up of strong, obvious, pure white or pure black shapes. There are no effects of mid-tones (greys) in this type of print.

In both types of relief print, the design has to be cut in reverse, like a mirror image, and a magnifying glass is used to view the section of the block being worked on. Large-scale blocks can take months to complete. Whatever is cut out of the block appears as an area of white in the final print and whatever is left of the original surface of the block prints black.

Each print is individually produced, by hand, by inking up the block and passing it, with the paper on top, through the roller press. Good quality fine-art papers are used which are quite heavy, so that the prints have a gently embossed appearance when they come off the press. The numbers of prints in each edition are limited as indicated and every print is signed and given its own edition number.

The development of one print

Facing is a series of proof prints which demonstrate the development of one of the prints illustrated – No.45, *The Hatchet Inn and its Surroundings*.

First, I made several sketches and took many photographs of this view from slightly different spots as I walked along Denmark Street towards the Inn. The final design is a combination of several different aspects, culled from these sources, which I hope gives a clearer sensation of the true context of the Inn than any one view could give.

Most importantly, I retained in my mind, and noted in my sketches, the sight of the Inn dramatically caught in the side light of a strong afternoon sun. Such vivid, visual sensations are often the vital trigger points which first make me keen to respond to a particular subject.

Next, by referring to my sketches, I drew out the design to the size I wanted to engrave it. I worked straight on to tracing paper so that I could transfer this sketch onto the vinyl block, by burnishing the back of the paper when it was placed over the block, with a wooden spatula. This automatically reverses the image, as required by this technique. After strengthening the resulting pencil image with a fine, black waterproof pen, the block was ready to start engraving.

With this particular print, I began with the lightest form in the whole composition, that of the Inn, which I intended to be the focal point of the design. For this, I used a fine V-shaped gouge to cut out the lightest areas and a fine graver or tint tool, used in traditional wood-engraving, for the more subtle details.

I tend to take proof (or trial) prints at regular intervals as I am working, or at least at the end of each session of engraving (which can go on for many hours). This allows for tonal and textural adjustments to be made as the work proceeds.

I then worked outwards from the Inn, using engraving tools to suggest textures of stucco, brick, asphalt and so on, as well as the patterns of roof tiles and slates. I knew these finer tools would produce tones which would remain subdued compared with those used for the Inn. The intention was to create a series of interesting and varied frames around the Inn but to retain it as the clear centre of attention.

Once the whole design was worked out in a preliminary fashion, the lengthy job of fine-tuning the overall tonal structure could begin. It is usually advisable to understate, initially, rather than to overstate; one can always remove more from the block to make an area lighter but it is almost impossible to make an area darker with this technique (I have sometimes been reduced to cutting out a whole area from the vinyl block and grafting in a fresh piece when things have gone seriously wrong but this is not an easy thing to do).

I spent a long time adjusting the light on the façade of the house on the left-hand side of the composition, trying to grade it so that it would seem as if caught in glancing sunlight but not compete with the stronger light falling on the façade of the Inn.

I hope the finished result captures some of the excitement I find in the juxtaposition of all these different styles of architecture.

Sequence of proof prints showing the development of *The Hatchet Inn and its Surroundings*.

1

The Docks from Redcliffe Wharf
to the Suspension Bridge

The Docks from Redcliffe Wharf to the Suspension Bridge

I have always derived much stimulus for my artwork from the city docks. These prints record some of my favourite spots along the floating harbour starting on the Grove, near St Mary Redcliffe, and then journeying as far as the Suspension Bridge. Some of these prints are based on sketches which date back several years, so they record things as they were rather than as they are now.

1 *Panorama of Bristol Docks 1995*

33 x 140 cms 13 x 55 ins

I drew this view from observation around the time I began experimenting with relief print-making but it was another two years before I felt I had sufficient skill to attempt to translate the large sketch into a print. One morning, I saw the view with a light fall of snow on it and realised the scene could be interpreted in just two tones: pure black and pure white. I used only lino-cutting gouges for this design. This was the first large-scale relief print I ever produced. It won a prize in the National Print show at the RWA in 1997.

It is interesting to see how many changes have occurred in this view since 1995.

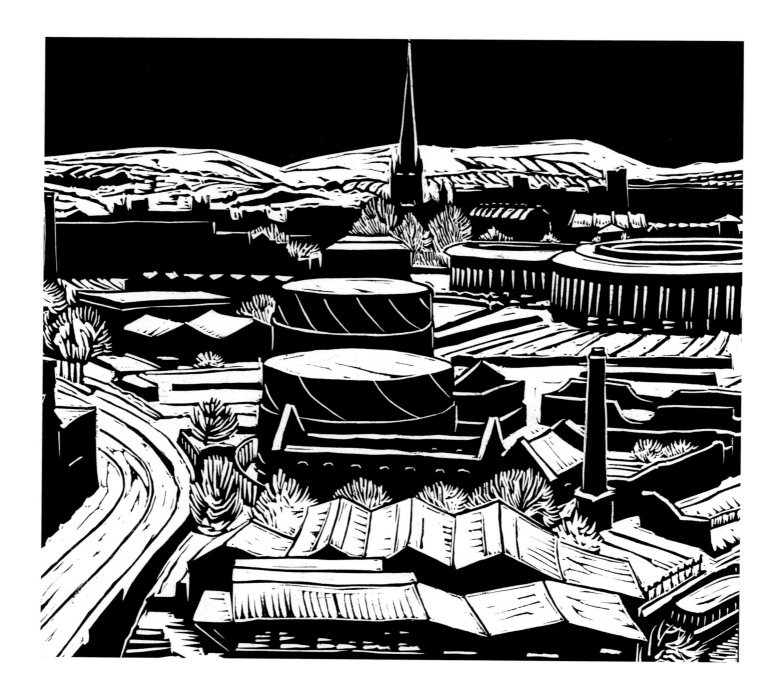

Two actual-size details of No. 1: the old gasworks and the ss *Great Britain*.

2 Redcliffe Wharf

17 x 48 cms 7 x 18 ¾ ins

I used a combination of lino-cutting gouges and wood-engraving tools for this design to achieve the variety of tone and texture I felt the subject called for. This has since become my preferred method of working for most subjects. This view from the Grove, looking towards St Mary Redcliffe, marks the starting point for my journey through the docks.

3 *Cranes on Prince's Wharf*
20 x 8 cms   8 x 3 ins

The strong silhouettes of these cranes
against the sky are striking. This view,
combining a bold foreground shape with
more delicate ones behind, and the abstract
play of positive and negative shapes
reminded me of some of the prints by the
Japanese masters, Hokusai and Hiroshige
whom I so admire.

4 *Old Timber-yard and Gasworks from Hotwell Road*

13.5 x 18 cms 5 1/2 ins x 7 1/4 ins

Graham's Timber-yard stood on the site of Lime Kiln Dock. I remember seeing timber being delivered here by ship when I first came to Bristol in the 1960s. The yard has gone, and this is now the site of a large apartment block development. Gas Ferry landing stage is on the right and St Mary Redcliffe is in the distance.

I have drawn and painted this scene many times over the years. I like the simple man-made forms and the way buddleia, that great opportunistic plant, strove to decorate them each summer.

5 *Dawn View from Hotwell Road looking towards Prince's Wharf*
13.5 x 18 cms 5¼ x 7¼ ins

This is drawn from the same spot as No.4. The *ss Great Britain* is just off the right-hand side. I was aiming for a back-lit effect with the sun just coming up and a rather still surface to the water.

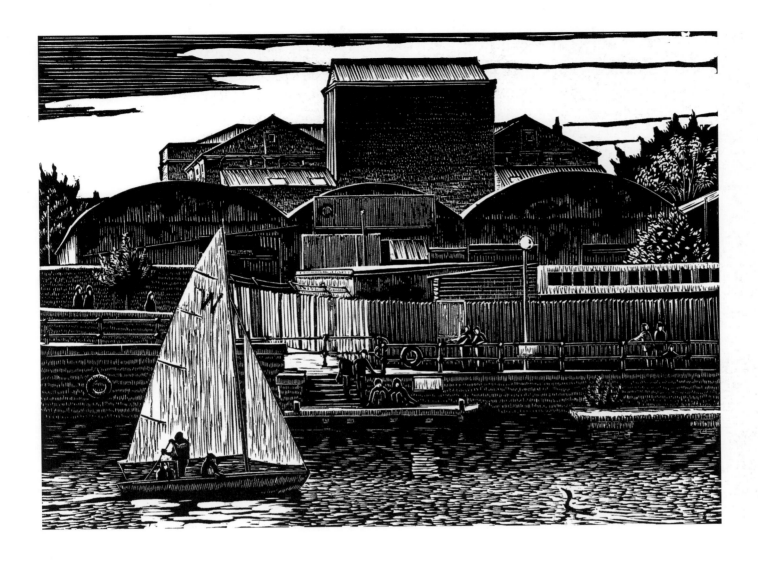

6 *The McArthur Warehouse and other buildings on Wapping Wharf*

13.5 x 18 cms 5 1/4 x 7 1/4 ins

Drawn from near the Gas Ferry landing stage. This combination of strong geometric forms clustered together reminds me of a still-life by Morandi. These red-brick industrial buildings have a grandeur all their own. The view may not exist for much longer, though, as developers have their eyes on this prime bit of real estate.

7 *Dawn View of the* ss **Great Britain** *from Hotwell Road*

17 x 48 cms 7 x 18¼ ins

Another view from the same spot as plate No.4. The filigree silhouette of the masts of the ship against the early morning sky and the still reflections disturbed only by the harbour-master's boat were very pleasing.

8 *The* ss Great Britain *and the* Matthew 2001
36 x 120cms 14 x 47ins

Another of my large prints. This was the view I used to have from the end of my garden, until it was obscured by recently built apartment blocks. I drew and painted this view many times over the thirty odd years I have lived here and I did this large-scale print as a means of commemorating (and bidding good-bye to) the view.

I moved in soon after the ss *Great Britain* had been returned to the dock where it was constructed and it was a pleasure to watch the rusting skeleton being steadily transformed into the majestic sight it is today. The replica of Cabot's ship, the *Matthew*, makes an attractive companion.

Two actual-size details of No. 8.

9 *The* ss Great Britain *and the* Matthew: *Snow*

6.5 x 21cms 2$\frac{1}{2}$ x 8$\frac{1}{2}$ ins

This is a miniature version of No.8.

10 *Docks View: The Funnel*

20.5 x 20.5 cms 8¼ x 8¼ ins

A close-up view where I was aiming to
emphasise the abstract play of black and
white shapes using only lino-cutting
gouges.

11 *Mooring Devices from around the Dock*
13.5 x 18 cms 5½ x 7¼ ins

The strong forms and weathered surfaces of
these implements are a pleasure to observe
all around the docks.

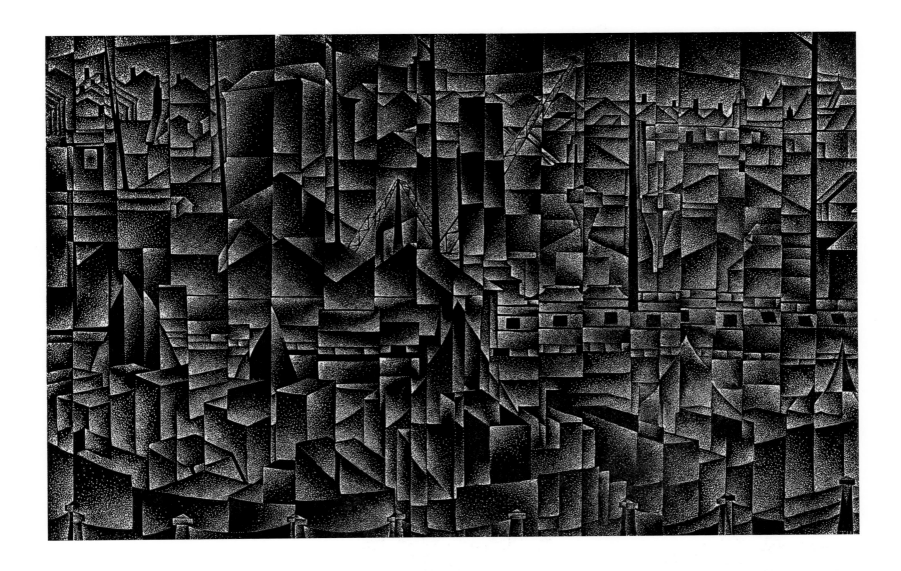

12 *Docks Abstract*

33 x 51 cms   13 x 20 ins

This is based on part of the view in No.8. The approach was influenced by cubist devices of disjunction and fragmentation. I used a wood-engraving tool called a round scorper in this and in the previous print, to produce the softly graded stippled effect.

It is an effective but very time-consuming method and in using it to produce a print of this size I almost felt I ran the risk of repetitive strain injury. I suspect that my desire to manipulate the subject in this way had more than a merely formal significance

in view of the fact that I engraved the block during the period when the subject was being gradually concealed from my sight.

13 *Cumberland Basin*

17 x 48 cms 7 x 18 3/4 ins

A panorama from near the splendid new bridge on Poole's Wharf with the bonded warehouses in the distance. The challenge, here, was to try to capture the effects of reflections using a variety of engraving tools.

14 *The Underfall Yard*

14x 18 cms 5$\frac{1}{2}$ x 7 ins

Another pleasing conglomeration of simple
geometric forms at this still-working end of
the docks.

15 *The Chimney*
21.5 x 6 cms 8½ x 2½ ins

An exercise in counter-change: light forms
against dark, dark forms against light.

Evening reflections at this end of the docks
can be fascinating.

16 *Clifton Suspension Bridge and Clifton from the Cumberland Basin*

28 x 120 cms 11 x 47 ins

This was the second large panorama I produced. It is the classic Bristol view which has attracted many artists to it ever since – and even before – the bridge was completed. I enjoyed recording the complexities of the buildings of Clifton and then being able to be freer in the handling of the trees to the left.

Two actual-size details of No.16.

2

CLIFTON AND CLIFTON WOOD

Clifton and Clifton Wood

This set of prints also represents a journey. This one starts on Cumberland Basin, moves along the dockside and then goes up through Clifton Wood and on to Clifton. The prints record some of the views and a few details of buildings which particularly appeal to me. I have often felt that Clifton Wood does not get enough attention in books on Bristol; so, in an attempt to remedy this, the emphasis is on that area, rather than on its already well-recorded neighbour.

17 *Panorama of Clifton Wood from the Cumberland Basin*

19 x 91.5 cms 7¹⁄2 x 36 ins

This view is from the fly-over, looking between the two bonded warehouses. There is a pleasing balance between attractive domestic architecture and trees and gardens from this vantage point. It is a spectacular entrance to the city from the south-west.

This is another large print as the subject seemed ideally suited to the panoramic format.

18 *Clifton Wood from Gas Ferry Road*

17 x 48 cms 7 x 18¾ ins

I always liked these houses on Southernhay Avenue with their steep gardens sweeping down to behind the buildings on Hotwell Road. In the foreground are ruined gasworks buildings and the ferry landing stage is below on the waterside.

This view can no longer be seen owing to the recent developments on the dockside.

19 *White Hart Steps, Clifton Wood*
21 x 6.5 cms 8¼ x 2½ ins

These old steps connect Belle Vue Crescent
and World's End Lane with the bottom of
Jacob's Wells Road. They still come as a
surprise to many people, even those who
have lived in the city a long time.
I have lived in a cottage on these steps for
over thirty years.

I sketched this view from high up on St
Peter's House which overlooks the steps.
It is difficult to believe this is just a few
minutes' walk from the city centre.

There is a pleasing, organic feeling to the
forms in this view and lots of interesting
detail. It was an enjoyable challenge trying
to record it all on such a small scale.

20 *Bristol Cathedral from World's End Lane*
13 x 18.5 cms 5 x 7 1/4 ins

This quaintly named lane is at the top of
White Hart Steps. The print is based on a
sketch I did many years ago, and it is no
longer possible to see the Cathedral from
this spot because the foliage on the left is
much thicker.

21 *Porch in Clifton Wood Road*
13 x 18.5 cms 5 x 7¹/₄ ins

There are a number of very decorative old porches in this road and no two are exactly alike.

This is my favourite. I find its relaxed lean against the stone building most appealing.

22 *White Cottage, Clifton Wood Road*

14 x 20 cms 5¹/₂ x 8 ins

The curvaceous shape of the Dutch gable-
end to this tiny cottage against the roof-
scape of the buildings beyond is very
striking. It is a surprise to note that only
the central rectangular window of the three
pointed-arch windows on the cottage is
real. The others are painted to look like
windows.

23 *Drinking Fountain, end of Birdcage Walk, St Andrew's Churchyard, Clifton*
13 x 18.5 cms 5 x 7 1/4 ins

Another interesting little detail of the area. 'Fear of the Lord is the fountain of life' reads the inscription in the alcove.

Clifton & Hotwells Improvement Society has a scheme to restore the fountain, along with the old churchyard behind.

While I was drawing this, the squirrel seemed to delight in playing hide-and-seek with the cat.

24 *Clifton Cathedral*

25.5 x 8 cms 10 x 3 ins

This is based on a sketch I did from the old
Art Room of Clifton High School where I
used to teach.

The elegant silhouettes of the trees
contrasted in a pleasing way with the bold,
simple modern architecture of the
cathedral. I felt I was being influenced by
Japanese prints, once more, in the way this
design developed.

25 *Clifton High School: the Main Building*

17 x 48 cms 7 x 18¾ ins

This imposing building is surprisingly well hidden, even though it is in the heart of Clifton. Its steep roof-scape is reminiscent of a French chateau. I always loved the grounds and especially the majestic copper beech tree.

I spent many interesting and enjoyable years as Head of Art & Design at Clifton High. I often used this façade as a drawing exercise for my pupils and helped many of them to turn their sketches into linocuts. I hope they will approve of this attempt.

26 *Fountain outside the Victoria Rooms, Clifton*

17 x 48 cms 7 x 18¾ ins

It is a joy to see this spectacular bronze
fountain working again. It is full of quirky
and amusing details and includes various
marine creatures which reveal themselves to
you only if you take an attentive walk
around the whole ensemble.

3

BRANDON HILL AND ENVIRONS

Brandon Hill and Environs

This is my local park and it always feels a great privilege to have such an amenity on my doorstep. It contains much of interest and its trees and gardens are beautifully maintained.

This set of prints records views of Brandon Hill from various vantage points in Clifton Wood and Park Street, as well as some details in the park itself and also some views of other parts of the city which can be seen from the slopes of the park.

27 *Panoramic View of Brandon Hill from Clifton Wood*

30 x 120 cms   12 x 47 ins

This is the third large-scale panorama I produced. The view was drawn from the end of Belle Vue Crescent. The backs of the houses on Constitution Hill are on the left.

Brandon House flats appear on the right. The dramatic sweep of the hill and the way the architectural forms relate to it attracted me to this view.

The Italianate Cabot Tower appears in many of my prints. (It is perhaps my equivalent of Mount Fuji in the prints of Hokusai and Hiroshige).

Two actual-size details of No.27.
Roseberry Terrace and Cabot Tower.

28 *Cabot Tower with Starry Sky*
   21 x 7 cms   8$^{1}\!/_{2}$ x 2$^{3}\!/_{4}$ ins

It is still possible to get a good view of the
stars on a really clear night, despite the
light pollution of the city.

The block needed to be very lightly
engraved to give the shimmering effect.
Careful inking is required to retain the
clarity of the image.

29 *Brandon Hill from Hill View in Clifton Wood*
40 x 29cms 15¾ x 11½ins

A view glimpsed between houses on Hill-
Side at the end of Belle Vue Crescent
looking towards the Field House on
Brandon Hill.

Once again, it was the combination of
natural forms and man-made ones and the
variety of textures in foliage and stonework
which attracted me to this subject.

30 *Panoramic View towards Queen Elizabeth Hospital School from the top of Jacob's Wells Road*
17 x 48 cms   7 x 18³/₄ ins

A wide-angle view drawn from the top of the multi-storey car park opposite the school. The new theatre building in the centre harmonises well with its surroundings and, from this angle, completes a satisfying arrangement of buildings leading the eye up to the tower.

31 *Wrought-iron Seat on Brandon Hill*
15 x 20 cms 6 x 8 ins

This seat used to be round an oak tree on the western slopes of the park in a perfect spot for watching the sunset. It was placed there when the tree was set in 1863, according to the plaque at the back of the seat. I passed by some time ago and workmen were removing the seat. They told me it was to be restored and enlarged but, so far, it has not reappeared. The completely soulless modern seat which has been sited nearby recently is surely not considered a worthy replacement for this Victorian one?

32 *The University Tower from Berkeley Square*
19 x 14 cms   7$\frac{1}{2}$ x 5$\frac{1}{2}$ ins

This square is just off Brandon Hill and I
have always liked this view in winter with
the tower seen through the network of bare
branches.

In this print, I copied a technique often
used by the Japanese printmakers when
they wanted to achieve the effect of looking
at an object through a screening device
such as the trees here. The tower and the
rest of the architecture were printed first
and then the trees were printed on top
from a second block.

33 *Constitution Hill from Brandon Hill*
21 x 21 cms   8¼ x 8¼ins

I like the various styles of the buildings, stacked one above the other, on this very steep hill. The Georgian terrace of Belle Vue is to the right. Hill-Side is to the left and the Old Police Station, now used by Bristol Wildlife Trust, is below.

34 *The Old Police Station, Jacob's Wells Road (now Bristol Wildlife Trust)*
13.5 x 18.5 cms 5¹/4 x 7¹/2 ins

This is the view from the bottom of
Constitution Hill, looking towards
Brandon Hill.

35 *The Old Swimming Baths on Jacob's Wells Road*
17 x 48 cms 7 x 18³/4 ins

This fine building with its Italianate façade is now used as a dance centre. It is not easy to step back far enough to appreciate it properly down on the road but there are better viewing points on Brandon Hill.

I used another wide-angle format because I wanted to include everything from the roundabout and St Peter's House at the lower end of the road, up to the bottom of Constitution Hill on the right.

36 *St George's, Brandon Hill*
17 x 48 cms 7 x 18³⁄4 ins

This was part of the view from a tall office block I visited on the Centre. The park gradually filters into the city from this vantage point. Charlotte Street and Great George Street lead off from it, above and below St George's. The buildings at the bottom edge are on Park Street.

37 *St George's, Brandon Hill*
8 x 20 cms 3 x 8 ins

Seen from a block of flats on Park Row, this
is another view of one of the city's most
popular concert venues.

4

AROUND THE CITY CENTRE AND BEYOND

Around the City Centre and Beyond

These prints record some of the old and
new sights which can be seen around the
central area of the city and a few which are
a little further out.

38 *Panoramic View of the Centre from Colston Tower*
32 x 120 cms 12½ x 47 ins

The fourth large-scale panorama I produced was completed in early 2000 and recorded part of the Centre as it was before recent and controversial redevelopment. Pero's Bridge is to the left, the Cathedral is in the centre and Brandon Hill is glimpsed at the top right. The sliding dome over the auditorium of the Hippodrome Theatre is in the almost exact centre of the print.

It was a challenge to make this view work because there are a number of buildings difficult to find attractive in themselves. I felt it would be possible, though, once I had seen the containing horse-shoe effect produced by the docks area on the left, following a curve round behind the Cathedral which then sweeps to the right through the Council House and Orchard Street. Working in black and white helps to impose a harmony on a scene which it might be hard to sense in actuality.

Two actual-size details of No. 38, one looking towards Narrow Quay, the other towards Orchard Street.

39 *Sail Sculpture on the Centre, Rainy Day*
20 x 8 cms   8 x 3 ins

I like this sculpture on the Centre, though
it is a pity that some of its plain white sails
have recently been replaced by advertisements.

This is another print which uses two blocks
– one for the sculpture and the figures, and
a second one, printed on top, for the rain.
I liked the way the sculpture was reflected
in the pavement on a rainy day.

40 *Part of the Cathedral School from College Green*
13 x 18.5 cms 5 x 7¹/₄ ins

This view always looks to me like a stage set. It is contained between the Cathedral on the left and the old archway next to the Central Library on the right. The archway leads down to the new Millennium Square development featured in the next three prints.

41, 42 *Two Views of the Planetarium on Millennium Square*
Each 13.5 x 18.5 cms 5 1/4 x 7 1/4 ins

This is a very beautiful new object in the city and the changing reflections on its mirror-surface are fascinating. It was intriguing trying to translate them in terms of engraving.

43 *Reflections in the @t Bristol Science Centre*
17 x 48 cms 7 x 18¾ ins

I think this development is a really
successful and exciting new addition to the
city. From this angle, the reflection of the
sail roof structure of the Imax cinema on
the façade of the science centre looks like a
gigantic winged creature, ready for take-off.

44 *Park Street in the Snow*
13.5 x 9.5 cms 5 1/4 x 3 3/4 ins

I tried to remove as little material as
possible from this block – just enough to
suggest the scene, looking up Park Street
from College Green.

45 *The Hatchet Inn and its Surroundings*

38 x 27 cms 15 x 10¾ ins

I have drawn close-up views of just the
Hatchet Inn in the past. On this
occasion, though, I tried to make a
workable design which not only included
the inn but also all the architectural
elements from other periods which
surround it.

The final composition is really a
combination of several slightly different
views seen when walking towards the
Hatchet along Denmark Street.

I have always liked the visual surprise this
building gives when it comes into view at
the end of the street.

46 *Christmas Steps and Park Row*
48 x 17 cms 18¾ x 7 ins

Another view from a tall office building where I tried to find some order in a complex area of the city containing many different styles of architecture piled one on top of the other. Christmas Steps lead up from the lower left to Colston Street and Park Row which cross at the top of the composition.

This is the largest vertical panorama I have produced.

47 *Old Buildings at the foot of Christmas Steps*
18.5 x 13.5 cms 7$\frac{1}{2}$ x 5$\frac{3}{4}$ ins

This is a more familiar view of the
buildings which appear at the bottom of
the previous print.

It is surely one of the most picturesque
views in the city. (The fish and chips are
reckoned to be among the best, too).

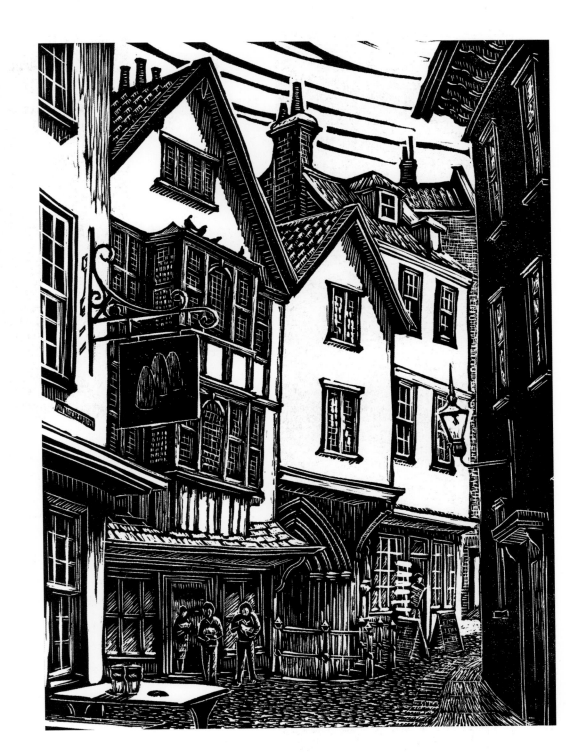

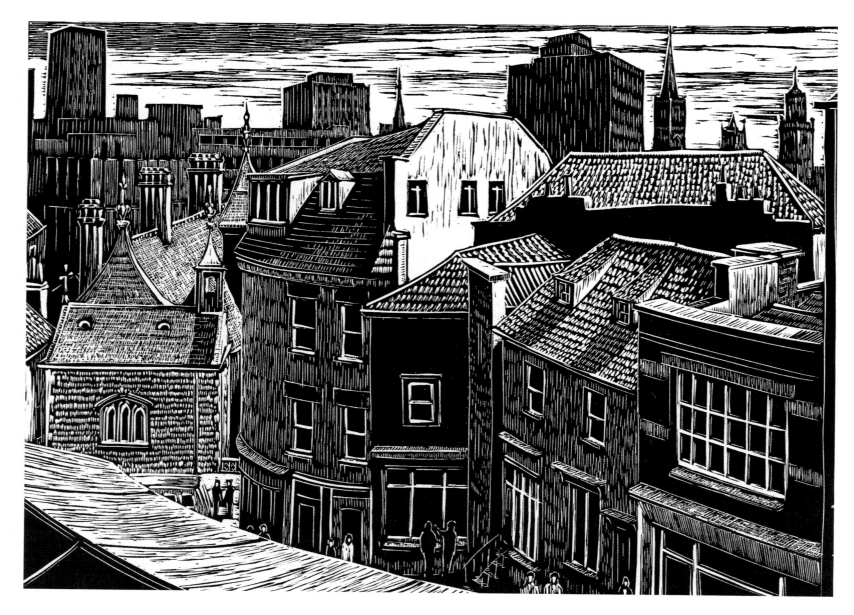

48 *Buildings on Lower Park Row*
15 x 20.5 cms 6 x 8³/₄ ins

I have drawn and painted this scene, looking down on to Lower Park Row, several times but this is my first engraving of it.

A number of the spires of city churches are visible from this spot. The top of Christmas Steps can be seen at the bottom left. I have always enjoyed drawing roof-scapes such as this which can be full of pleasing and unplanned juxtapositions of forms.

49 *Park Row and St Michael's Hill*
33 x 51 cms 13 x 20 ins

This is another view, seen from the uppermost floor of an office block on the Centre. St Michael's Hill is in the middle with the Bristol Royal Infirmary and the new Children's Hospital to the right. The roofs of the buildings at the bottom of Christmas Steps are glimpsed in the bottom left-hand corner.

50 *Buildings on Victoria Street*
17 x 48 cms 7 x 18¾ ins

I found this series of buildings from the
Temple Church, with its leaning tower,
down to the Shakespeare Inn full of interest
and variety. Victoria Street is on the route
out of the city towards Bath.

51 *Totterdown from the Bath Road*
17 x 48 cms 7 x 18³/4 ins

This is an area of the city usually only glimpsed from a car or bus as one enters or leaves the city. I like the way the buildings echo the forms of the hillside and the verdant sloping gardens of the houses. Its name is a perfect description of the area.